Best Wishes
t the Battlefield Tour
x

for Karen Kata
x

MOODS, MOMENTS & MEMORIES

MOODS
MOMENTS
& MEMORIES

POETRY BY

KEN KITSON

BANK HOUSE BOOKS

First published in the United Kingdom in 2009 by
Bank House Books
PO Box 3
NEW ROMNEY
TN29 9WJ UK

www.bankhousebooks.com

Cover photograph by Dani Batty
Ken Kitson biography worded by Helen Tidswell

British Library Cataloguing in Publication Data
A catalogue record for this book is available from the British Library

ISBN 9781904408611

Typesetting and origination by Bank House Books
Printed by Lightning Source

Ken Kitson Biography

Ken Kitson is a British actor who has been active on British television since the early 1970s and is currently best known for playing the policeman PC Cooper in the BBC's long-running series *Last of The Summer Wine* , which Ken has been in for twenty-seven years.

Ken spent three years at East 15 Acting School, where he was coached by Ian McKay and was subsequently awarded a Stage Fighting and Fencing Diploma with recommendations. He then went on to teach fencing and unarmed combat at the National Theatre, Royal Court, London, and various other London theatre schools. After actor training Ken's early roles included working alongside Norman Wisdom, and his first lead role came in 1974 for London Weekend Television, in *A Wish for Wally's Mother.* The start of a lengthy career for Ken had begun, seeing him cast for over 250 TV roles in shows such as *The Bill, Ruth Rendell's Mysteries, Minder* and *The Sweeney.* Ken appears in the record books as the only actor to have appeared in *Coronation Street* four times as four different characters. Film appearances for Ken include *Brassed Off, When Saturday Comes* and as Giant Rumblebuffin in the BBC's *The Lion, The Witch and The Wardrobe.* Ken's TV commercials have seen him as the genie for Mansfield Bitter, the lorry driver in the Heinz Tomato soup advert, and dressed in a rabbit costume as a children's entertainer for a Del Monte advert. The list is endless!

You can view Ken's show reels on his Youtube channel, which can be found at

http://www.youtube.com/watch?v=Kq2E0sOwCS0&feature=channel.

Ken's career has also led him into directing and running his own drama class in Wilsden, Bradford, for fifteen years. He has also spent many years fundraising for his forthcoming film *Fistful of Dreams,* which he has scripted.

Writing poetry has been a love throughout Ken's life, and the poems in this book span his entire career. He finds his inspiration in real views, thoughts and feelings, to create poetry that readers can easily relate to.

Ken is proud to showcase illustrations from talented local artists, who have interpreted a selection of his poems.

CONTENTS

ALOHA PEOPLE

As I gaze, awash with the sea of faces,
All shapes and sizes and varying races,
The colours that hit you and the ones that blend,
A stream of footprints to which there's no end.
To look in their eyes as they pass my way,
Each one with their own story, if only to say.
The yachts in the harbour amid rippling waves,
Their masts to the sky, open sea each one craves.
The splendid array of canvas and hulls,
Displaying personal titles, owners enjoying lulls.
The buildings that surround them, stately and clean,
Looking down at the boats, wondering where they've been.
The tourists finding their favourite bars,
Staring out at the ocean, then up to the stars.
The fish in the water both large and small,
Attract all ages, swimming by the sea wall.
I'd better pay for my drinks before I forget,
Reaching into my pocket to cover the debt.
Walking back to my room, catching every open face,
New people tomorrow, most of today's no trace.

ILLUSTRATION BY HELEN KNOWLES

1

WHAT IS LOVE?

Love is the truth spoken, with the unspoken word,
Voices in your head, for you only to be heard,
Knowing they are faithful, however far apart,
You've become as one, guarding each other's heart.
Real love can only be felt for persons one to one,
Sometimes it's so painful you wish it had never begun.
To protect yourself from this hurt is impossible to do,
Man has tried from beginning of time, still they have no clue.
It has been said the world revolves around this feeling of
    love,
Many religious people say it comes from beyond and
    above.
Whatever the answer is, it's recommended to one and all,
There is no feeling like it when you truly fall.

It may start with a look from afar, but mostly when you are
    near,
You need to reach out and touch them, to you it's perfectly
    clear.
A few gentle words could be the next thing that between
    you passes,
In a crowded room wherever it be, you tend to ignore the
    masses.
Your eyes will meet and scan the being of this wonderful
    creation,
The joy that this brings you, is shared by everyone
    throughout the nation.
Your first tender kiss will tell you what you already know,
The touch of their hand excites you, and this you are sure
    will grow.
An arranged meeting is what's called for, the next step this
    must be,
To be alone with this person, yet you want all the world to
    see.

ILLUSTRATION BY CHRISTINE WILLAN

The waiting for this to happen seems like an eternity to unfold,
Could be inside, outside, sunshine, pouring rain or bitter cold,
It doesn't matter what the weather, it's the warmth you feel within;
To see them arrive makes you grow, a relationship you must begin.
You were right first time when that look between you did exchange.
Am I caring too fast? I don't think so, let us the next date arrange.
After this, the days, weeks and months are stolen with this emotion,
You live your life for another and you hope they have the same notion.
The times apart are filled thinking of magic places you both could go,
When you meet some you may see, more important your love to show.
To grow together, seeking honesty, truth and loving trust,
On this you lay your foundation, this building is a must.
There will be moments with your love when cracks appear in the stone,
But the two of you can repair the damage, knowing you're not alone.
All the obstacles can be overcome if the love you feel is deep enough,
This may sound selfish, but what the hell, who said life isn't tough?
To deny true love and happiness is an unwritten and punishable crime:
If you allow this to occur then you could sentence yourself for all time.

A total giving can strip you bare; then you're vulnerable,
  this is true,
But if the partner you've chosen is right, the rewards are
  enormous for you.
The sharing you have will grow in abundance each passing
  day,
From that first look, until one or both of you becomes old
  and grey.

So to fall in love is something we should all experience in
  our life,
The hurt, the pain, the passion, true joy between husband
  and wife.
Some may not marry, it's not important, the commitment is
  just the same,
As long as you're true, understanding and caring, love is
  not a game.
It's a hard road you have walked upon, and you'll arrive at
  many a junction,
Without the pitfalls and terrific heights, this amazing love
  won't function.
So take the plunge both feet first, never mind just wetting
  your toes,
Once you're wet you'll become dry, now you're two with the
  one you chose.

COUNTY SCARS

The sombre dark stone houses rising up to the sky,
Tarmac roads and streets disturbed from when new.
Reservoirs half empty, despite the rainfall are dry;
Waiting for that overdue bus arriving, there are two.
Each piece of land, no matter the size, immediately built on,
Mills torn down to make way for houses and parking cars,
Green fields trampled from heavy machinery, animals gone.
Does anybody stop to think awhile, to look at the county scars,
The people losing pride in the towns and also in their work,
Littered pavements of fast food wrappers, and that infernal dog muck;
Suddenly it's trendier not to have a job, it's easier to shirk.
These things could all be put right if we just pause and take a look.
The outlying countryside has still kept most of its charm,
Hills and mountains, waterfalls and streams, are still a wondrous sight,
Hopefully visitors taking in these views will keep it from pollution and harm.
They are there for eternity, our children to come, one day we'll see the light,
Despite all man has done to spoil this grand old wool town.
To live anywhere else and lose one's roots, for now I will defer,
Concrete, progress, overshadowed, by friends not letting you down,
So let's take pride, try to keep it clean, our lovely county Yorkshire.

ILLUSTRATION BY CHRISTINE WILLAN

GOOD TIMES

We were always together,
As kids we were one,
There for each other
In a world full of fun.

These were the good times, good times,
Wonderful days, in a magical haze.
Good times, good times,
Nursery rhymes and fantasy plays.

As the years passed on by
And into our teens,
It became harder to try,
Remembering we're friends.

Why must it be,
The older we get,
One usually breaks free;
How could we forget?

These were the good times, good times,
Wonderful days, turned to worrying haze.
Good times, good times,
Why have the rhymes become tragedy plays?

Now we are married, family of five,
Places that mattered are lacking of life.
Where are the ice lollies, trees we used to climb,
Coming home with grazed knees? Please come back for all time.

VOCATIONS OF LIFE

A Joiner of People,
A Mechanic of Life,
A Driver for Peace,
Engineer against Strife,

An Actor with Passion,
Upholsterer of Dreams,
Designer of Fashion,
A Planter of Trees.

Let's all, let's all,
Let's all unite as one;
Let's do, let's do,
Let's do what has to be done.

A Composer of Music,
An Author of Plays,
Landlord for the Needy,
Pet Lover for Strays,

A Broadcaster of News,
A Singer of Songs,
A Painter of Views,
They all Right the Wrongs.

A FRIEND

A friend is a person in whom you can trust,
One you can turn to in your hour of need,
If you're down on your luck and just want a
crust,
They're a phone call away; they'll give you a feed.

A friend may lend you money, even their last pound,
Or a shoulder to cry on, a sympathetic ear,
They'll give you advice when they come round,
Listening to troubles, not embarrassed when seeing a tear.

Share what you have for a friend who's without hope,
It helps you feel peace within your being.
Without friends in life we could not cope,
A friend's here, there, everywhere, all seeing.

If we have in this life six friends we can call,
Then we are rich beyond belief.
We can be proud, feeling oh! so tall,
Alone, we're a tree never bearing a leaf.

You can discuss with a friend whatever's on your mind,
Even though they may not always agree.
When you're stressed and tense they'll help you unwind,
Problems grow smaller, they have the key.

If a friend lets you down, then look for the cause,
When they are true it's not done in haste.
The one all-round rule is, there are no laws,
Don't jump to conclusions; to lose them is such a waste.
You can cry, you can laugh, or even show rage,
There are no bounds to where you can go
From the womb to the tomb, old or young of age,
When they're not with you they're there, and you know.

We can love them, we can hate them, till the end of our
    days,
The disagreements and silly fallouts are all pages
In the book of life we all read, then light turns to greys,
Love lays you to rest, memories live on through the ages.

So this is a friend, with just a few things you share,
It varies from one friend to another what they do,
The essential thing in life is to show you really care,
Never forgetting old friends for pastures new.

HOW THE WORM TURNS

There's a certain breed of people who fool you all the way,
No matter what the reason you still get taken for a ride,
A smile, a gesture, a compliment, you listen to what they say,
Pretending friendship behind the mask they all hide.

You're there for them in many ways, but they still stab you in the back,
Friendly towards you when it suits their purpose and need,
But you fall for it every time, not seeing the character they lack,
Thinking they're honest and true, not full of malice and greed.

They play you off against one another to satisfy their needs,
Not caring what hurt they do, the lasting suffering.
It's of no consequence the damage caused by their malicious deeds,
All this to get what they want, never once apologising.

You resent being bitter, not trusting those who are true;
Despite all your efforts, the doubts in other people still remain.
The twisted truths, black being the colour painted about you;
These persons are clever, it's a fact, hope it won't happen again.

Now everything has a way of turning full circle, it's been said,
Every now and then they get what's due, and that's great.
You stop believing in them, you're not as easily misled,
They need you first, start losing friends; I suppose it's fate.

ILLUSTRATION BY ANDREA STEVENSON

YOUNG, OLD, THEN OUT IN THE COLD

When a man gets to become older in years,
But still is young in body, soul and mind,
Told, settle down, as another birthday nears,
Well make a fool of yourself, if so inclined.

He begins to take a close look at himself,
As he sits alone in his favourite chair.
Are they right, will I end up on the shelf,
At the end of the day, does anyone care?

Young women whom he's in contact with now and again,
Do not understand how his emotions may stir,
When he's with them, kissed on the cheek yet again,
Not realising the arousing that this could incur.

A man relies on basic instinct from an early age,
The signs are there, he's positive, he's not wrong.
He moves in, there's no going back at this stage,
She flirts, the level of her attention is still strong.

They have a laugh, a terrific night was had by all,
What's age, he thinks, it's how people feel that matters.
She smiles at him, making him proud and extra tall,
He steals a kiss. Disaster. Yes, the bubble shatters.

He caught his image, turned away, what a sad old joke,
She's so beautiful, he wants to turn back the hands of time.
Driving home, little talk, never a true word was spoke,
A lesson learnt: loving younger is obviously such a crime.

Journey home seems longer, silence goes on forever,
At last they're home, turn sharp left by the school.
Another kiss on the cheek, he's not feeling very clever,
Words ringing in his ears, 'No fool like an old fool'.

He locks his door, kettle on, and sits in his old armchair,
Reflecting on the evening, once again he's so alone.
What was he thinking, he didn't possibly have a prayer,
Silence broken, her voice: 'thanks' on the answerphone.

S Tidswell 9/09

16

STRESS

A body can take so much stress,
To extract more would be under duress.
Relaxing the mind is not easy to do,
For most of us these are deserts new.
Each new thought is not always clear,
Therefore the way forward we may fear.
To close your eyes and empty your head
Needs amazing control, harder done than said.
The rigour of life takes its toll on our being,
Sapping your strength, when you're not seeing.
This dilemma to combat, we must take time out,
Otherwise our muscles will have reason to shout.
There's no one set rule, but ponder this thought,
A loved one's help, through hard times we're brought.
So take stock of your life, ease up the strain,
Take heed this warning, be strong, fight again.

ILLUSTRATION BY SUSAN TIDSWELL

EH! ARE YOU LISTENING?

My Mum's a never-ending song that I'd love to turn off,
She's at me day and night; God, living here is naff,
I can't do a thing that's right, it really is a drag,
It's one endless boring fight. Nag, nag, nag, nag, nag.

'All you do is watch the telly, why don't you go out for a walk?
Your room is dirty, very smelly; I'm fed up with hearing myself talk.
Your hair is manky, will you move your feet.
God, use a hanky, you're such a deadbeat.'

Are you listening, are you listening, are you listening to me?
Are you listening, are you listening? Eh! Are you listening to me?

'You said you're not on drugs, and you want me to believe you.
Those mates of yours are thugs, your exam results are due.
Take those videos back, you've had them over a week.
What's wrong with the vac? How long's your trainers had a leak?'

'Pull yourself together, I shan't tell you again,
God, I hate this weather, you're driving me insane.
I said you're staying in, you still haven't cleaned your room.
Do you have to make that din? Are you listening? I'm your mum!'

THE EMPTY HOUSE

The walls they are yellow,
The woodwork is all black,
The ceilings more mellow,
Harlequin chairs that attack.

Kitchen cupboards are green,
Quarry tiles on the floor,
Different designs to be seen,
Entering through louvre door.

One display on the walls,
Is assorted coloured tiles,
Pleasing to everyone who calls,
Releasing very broad smiles.

Terracotta carpets adorn
The floors and the stairs,
A new home has been born,
Removing all the past layers.

The bathroom shows style,
There are many features.
Glance at the mirror awhile,
At the two loving sea creatures.

Now the bedroom has class,
Wardrobes black, trimmed white,
With picture of a lovely lass
To whom I say goodnight.

The crowning glory must be,
Where two minds, together as one,
A full breakfast all to see,
A work of art and so much fun.

The house is now complete,
Transformed from old to new.
Everything truly works a treat,
The only thing missing is you.

BELIEF

No, I'm not a religious person,
I believe in something, that's for certain.
Strange events that we've all known,
And maybe, like some of you, proof to be
shown.
Faith or not, we all mention God's name,
Things going right or wrong, it's spoken all the same,
'Thank God' for the true happiness I feel,
Then pleading with him because of life's ordeal.
Back to a child when nothing clouded your mind,
Innocent in learning, storing every find,
Stories in the Bible, your eyes open wide.
How wonderful believing the truth will abide,
Like Santa with reindeer that fly through the air,
With bottomless toy sack, long beard and white hair.
Sadly belief comes to an end when years you age,
Fables and dreams don't read the same on the page.
These tales started somewhere, no-one can explain,
Thanks to whatever they will always remain,
The loved ones we've lost, accepting they're gone,
But deep down hoping, there's a place they move on.
So finally how can we say we don't partly believe?
When we look at our lives some dPoubts we relieve.

FRUITS OF LIFE

Love and happiness is not for the chosen few,
It's there for everyone, that's me and you.
The joy and vision you see, the warmth you feel,
Like the inner fruit when you remove the peel.

It's not a big house and plenty of land,
Fast cars anew, or servants on command,
Holidays abroad or a Caribbean cruise.
If this is your idea of happiness then you'll lose.

Love you soon will find
Is something you left behind,
Also it's in front of you,
It's there within your view.

Forget all the material things in life.
If you have children and a loving wife
You don't need more than what you have,
Happiness you feel when loved ones laugh.

All the money on God's soil
Can't buy happiness without toil,
Enjoy the excitement you first felt within
When you chose the fruit and peeled back the skin.

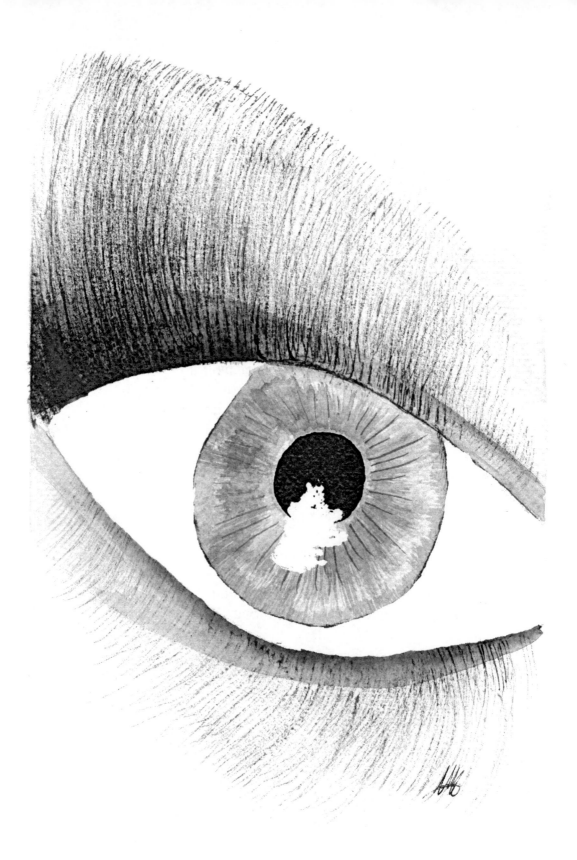

HEAD AND HEART

Heart says yes, head says no,
Heart says stay, head says go.
Heart says truth, head says lies,
Heart says ok, head just cries.
Heart says real, head says pretence,
Heart says action, heads says defence.
Heart says answers, head says questions,
Heart says believe, head says suggestions.
Heart says love, head says grief,
Heart says future, head disbelief.
Heart says tied, head says sever,
Heart says together, head says never.
Heart says two, head says none,
Heart says here, head says gone.

ILLUSTRATION BY ALEX MENSTON

Heart says trust, head says unsure,

Heart says safe, head says insecure.

Heart says family, head says alone,

Heart says honesty, head can't condone.

Heart says clear, head says foggy,

Heart says sure, head says groggy.

Heart says clean head says mess,

Heart says more, head says less.

Heart says listen, head says close,

Heart says warm, head just froze.

Heart says young, head says old,

Heart says feeling, head says cold.

Heart says certain, heads says tricked,

Heart says unhurt, head says kicked.

Heart says well, head says ill,

Heart says now, head says until.

Heart says poetry, head says phrases,

Heart says draw, head just erases.

Heart says think, heads says thought,

Heart says unbound, head says caught.

Heart says vision, head says blank,

Heart says swim, head says sank.

Heart says pure, head says rough,

Heart says thank you, head says enough.

Heart says colours, head says greys,

Heart says happy, head just dismays.

Heart says complete, head says tatters,

Heart says solid, head just shatters.

Heart says forever, head says apart,

Heart says head, head says heart.

JOURNEYING AT HOME

When the glass of the window
Is sheeted with rain,
And rooftops on show
Between drops that remain,

You look to yourself
In your cosy armchair,
In the atlas you delve,
You have to be where.

The world is your oyster
Or so it is told,
A pearl in a whisper
As secrets unfold.

Your eyes scan the countries,
All the sights you must see,
Remembering the journeys,
The years you were free.

Concentration is broken
By the silence outside,
The sun has awoken,
The windows have dried,

The book is replaced,
Footsteps are near,
The love in her face;
Your freedom, she's here.

ILLUSTRATION BY PAUL PARKES

WHAT IS IT?

There is an invasion in my head that suddenly I heard,
Or was it the calls you made, however trivial or absurd?
Is it a violent storm making my sleep to be broken,
Or was it in a dream where to me you had spoken?
Rain that is so heavy I can hear each shattered drop,
Or was it your words to me, enforcing my slumber to stop?
Wind howling against windows, penetrating every place,
Or was it your eyes engaging my own personal space?
Trees rustling and being bent to very near breaking,
Or was it a point I didn't understand that you were making?
Litter tossed around like leaves outside my dwelling,
Or was it the whispers of love that you were telling?
The sound of cars on wet roads for me to hear,
Or was it the wonderful promises you spoke so clear?
Doors and windows creaking with the storm brewing outside,
Or was it the love you showed me, the first time to confide?
The water flowing from the rooftops like a never-ending stream,
Or is it the tremendous urge to come and share my dream?
I hear the storm is over; all is calm and serene for me,
Or is it that you're always there, in my thoughts forever be?

ILLUSTRATION BY SIMON WRAY

STUFF OF DREAMS

Is it wrong to have a dream of more than one,
Or wait till one is over before the next is begun?
There is no rule in life saying you can't have maybe three,
Especially if no harm is done by wishing, surely you agree.
The fantasies and dreams you carry throughout the years
Come as a great surprise if the opportunity then appears.
They could be material things or something involving a friend,
Whatever these special thoughts, you hope a rewarding end.
You struggle every day to make these dreams come true,
Despite the cost and ridicule, you know they're right for you.
Magic moments can happen when you least expect,
To not grab them at this time is certainly neglect.
The two things definite in this world are death and birth,
So all the space between you must enjoy for all it's worth,

In spite of all our ups and downs, most come through with
    flying hues,
So aim high for the goals you have; they may become
    headline news.
From an early age we wish Santa to bring that special gift
On Christmas morning; to see it there, gives your heart a
    lift.
But as we grow older these are replaced by money and
    cost;
Our dreams are cars and castles – needing ownership, we
    are lost.
Although most people crave for these pricey goods and
    wares,
Some read up every day what's happened to their stocks
    and shares,
There are few of us left thinking of career and house,
And that one loving person to share it with, your spouse.
So yes, I'm like most I suppose, dreaming of this and that,
Some of them I will achieve; if not, a place to hang my hat.

FIGHTING THE MOOD

There's a mood in the air
That can lead to despair;
There's a feeling abroad
Makes you take the wrong road.

Which way do you turn now?
There will be a path somehow.
Everything you put your hand to
Disappears like the morning dew.

Just take stock of your life,
All your troubles and strife,
Make a list against and for,
Then merely tot up the score.

The decision is yours, right,
Nothing gained without a fight,
So pick yourself up from the boots,
Think on way back to your roots.

When you face trouble head on,
Then the battle's half won,
No more head in the sand,
Take life firmly by the hand.

If you believe in just one thing,
Then build on that and make it sing.
Step by step move up a stair,
Where it will end you know not where.

Your life is gaining strength,
Like swimming a breadth and then a length.
Build and build, and then build some more,
Never again will you be on the floor.

Life's what you make it, or so it goes,
You take the chances, highs and lows,
Nothing is given to you on a plate,
So get off your arse before it's too late.

Once ideas are flowing again,
The foundation is solid and will remain.
Now the mood in the air that led to despair
Has gone forever, like a dreadful nightmare.

Onward and upward, let's reach for the moon,
There's no stopping you now, with life you're in tune.
It's hard to relate to the mood you were in,
Don't ever return there; it would be a sin.

Now that your life's in order and rhyme,
We know it has taken effort and time.
You're ready to move on and assist others,
The knowledge you've gained for sisters and brothers.

You'll always remember the feeling you had,
And look back in amazement at what made you sad.
Never again, put those dark days behind you,
Like this poem from the beginning you just grew and grew.

WAITING

We wait for local buses,
We wait for passenger trains,
Others wonder what the fuss is,
The frustration still remains,
We wait in a supermarket,
We wait to get our food,
We wait for the car to park it,
We then develop a mood,
We wait for important calls,
We wait in waiting rooms,
We wait within four walls,
Men wait to be bridegrooms,
We wait for the elusive waiter,
We wait for that needed drink,
We wait for it to arrive later,
Why we do it, it makes you think,

We wait for the gas and electric man,
We wait for phones to be connected,
We wait for our eggs to boil in a pan,
We wait and hope we'll be respected,
We wait in reply to our letters,
We wait for our babies to be born,
We wait to become go-getters,
While we wait to grow forlorn,
We wait outside the pictures,
We wait for our photographs,
We wait for the football fixtures,
We wait for the punch-line laughs,
We wait for the taxi queue,
We wait for a clear blue sky.
I wait for all these things like you,
But we're reluctant to wait to die.

ILLUSTRATION BY ALEX MENSTON

ALONE IN LOVE

As I lay on my bed watching shadows on the wall,
Feeling so alone, wishing a deep sleep to fall.
The endless nights I have spent, living with just a
memory,
Did you share that time with me, or once again
fantasy.
The shadows moved and disappeared, a cool breeze
touched my face,
Turning my head I saw you there, like a fragile piece of
lace.
You smiled at me, not a spoken word, as you slipped
beneath the sheet,
Your cool skin brushing my warm thigh, I longed our lips to
meet.
As the moments ticked by our two bodies became more as
one,
Was this real, should I pinch myself, had another fantasy
begun?
I ran my fingers across your neck, then tiptoed down your
spine,
Suddenly you trembled, moved up close, this night I knew
you were mine.
Your hands moved slowly, caressing the parts until now to
you were unknown,
You kissed my cheek, I felt complete, with the love for me
you'd shown.
I held you tight, then kissed your neck, placed one hand
upon your thigh,
You responded quick, squeezed my buttocks hard,
followed by a pleasing sigh.
From that magical moment on a thousand kisses flowed
like rain,
I kissed your eyes, your nose, your ears, your whole body,
nothing did remain.

ILLUSTRATION BY ALEX MENSTON

When kissing your breast your reaction was purring,
     nipples stood firmly proud,
With my lips I moved down caressing between your thighs,
     you gave a cry out loud.
Your hand moved around between my legs; when you held
     me you stirred my whole being.
I ran my finger through the soft curly hair to a place that is
     usually unseen,
Then gently ventured inside you, parting moist lips of
     velvet,
Whilst in your hand 'he's beautiful' you whispered, the first
     drops I did submit.

As dawn drew near, with tenderness not one inch of our
     bodies unexplored,
We both knew the way forward, and the inevitable could not
     be ignored.
The heat of our bodies, they were welded as one, we
     enjoyed each other so much,
Your skin tasted salty, you slid down my chest, your mouth
     my penis did touch.
In ecstasy under your spell, then a pulsating sensation
     came from down below,
You had the same feeling, a firm grasp, preventing the
     explosion to grow.
We waited a while savouring our whole night of joy
     together,
I knew how I felt, and hoped you too needed it to last
     forever.
Then came the moment I entered your beautiful body all
     glowing,
Making such tender love, despite not a word, we were both
     knowing.
Every possible way we made love that night, no barriers
     between the two,
After all the pleasure, emotion and passion, we cuddled 'til
     morning anew.

I brushed my hand through your hair; your movement was
    slight,
Our eyes smiled at each other, reflecting on the night.
You turned to my face, nuzzled your head on my shoulder,
I reached down the bed, replacing the duvet, it's colder.
Then a strange experience came over me, and I'll never
    know the reason why,
Still holding you close, like a part of me, my eyes began to
    cry.
The tears rolled down and touched your cheek; you drank
    them 'til they were no more,
You kissed my lips, my neck, my chin, my eyes 'til they
    were no longer sore.

My dreams were good, my fantasies real, they were all so
    clear to me,
A night as this has got to be true, my eyes opened and then
    I see,
An empty space beside my hand, looking round the room
    in the light of day.
I see your shape, or is it a shadow, then the gentle words
    'You have a wonderful way'.

A PLEASURE TO BE GUILTY

If it's a crime to care for someone,
Especially gazing on them from afar,
Not suggesting anything that makes them run,
Admiring their beauty as they enter the bar,

Then guilty as charged,
Facts, somewhat enlarged.

If it's a crime to open a car door
For a lady young or old of years,
Expecting women to be feminine in what they wore,
Giving compliments as she first appears,

Then guilty as hell,
And time will tell.

If it's a crime to pull out a chair
For a partner or friend when dining out,
Or to count to ten as you're about to swear,
And order for both, when the waiters about,

Then guilty as sin,
And you just can't win.

If it's a crime to buy a lady flowers,
For no other reason than she likes them,
To offer shelter in those heavy showers,
And listen with interest to a problem,

Then guilty as can be,
And you'll never ever agree.

ILLUSTRATION BY ANDREA STEVENSON

Now if your crime is done from the heart,
And all these gestures with love are given free,
Because it's in your nature and of you it's a part,
Taught from an early age, cost of good manners, no fee,

Then not guilty as charged,
And yes the facts were enlarged,
Then not guilty as hell.
We all hope time will tell,
And certainly not guilty as sin,
Because good manners will always win.
So therefore not guilty as can be,
If you all think about the crimes you'll agree.
I rest my case for etiquette and respect,
Not taking one's partner for granted and in vain.
There's no room in this world to show a person neglect,
So look forward to when you can commit these crimes
   again.

HOW TO CLEAN MY WINDOWS

When the windows of life have lost their lustre,
And an occasional sparkle is all you can
muster,
No amount of water can clean the dull panes,
However hard you try, the cloudiness still
remains.
Taking a dry cloth to the glass seems to do the trick,
But when this is removed the fogginess is still thick.
So you think of something new to make them become clear;
Even though they are transparent, you can still see a
smear.
More liquid arrives from where you know not,
Although now it takes strength, every ounce you've got.
The cloth is now wet, once again you don't succeed
To get the result, and this now you surely need.
Maybe the best thing is from the problem to walk away,
Try to get some rest and tackle it the next day.
Practically asleep, the haziness is there once more,
Now you're lost for ideas of how to handle this chore;
So you rise from your bed and make another drink,
There must be a way, come on, look harder and think.
This enigma has lasted so long and is now in keeping,
Oh! Please someone help me to stop this heart-wrenching
weeping.

EXPLODING?

feeling

OVERLOADING

MEMORIES, ERODING...

FULL CIRCLE

Ideas Growing
Thoughts Flowing,
Brain Exploding,
Memories Eroding,
Mind Overloading,
Head Imploding,
Sight Confusing,
Eyes Refusing,
Questions Unceasing,
Answers Decreasing,
Time Unending,
Age Impending,
Ears Unhearing,
Speech Endearing,
Hands Feeling,
Heart Dealing,
Arms Cuddling,
Words Muddling,
Partners Adoring,
Others Ignoring,
Life Moving,
Love Soothing,
Seeds Sowing,
Ideas Regrowing.

ILLUSTRATION BY DANI BATTY

STOP PUSHING

Stop pushing, I said I'm OK,
I don't need you both night and day.
Stop pushing, you're driving me mad,
You'll spoil everything that we ever had.

    Stop pushing, I need some space,
    Don't make me forget your face.
    Stop pushing or I'll open the door,
    Please can't we be as we were before?

        Don't push, you're doing it again,
        Don't push, don't push me.
        Don't push, you're losing a friend,
        Don't push, don't push me.

Stop pushing, don't turn me away,
Our black and white is becoming grey.
Stop pushing, or we'll be at an end,
How many times do I say, there is no blend.

The pushing stopped but so have we,
We can't go on, you must agree.
The pushing stopped like a breath of fresh air,
I know it's too late, but I still care.

Pushing's stopped or am I mistaken,
I know you're feeling forsaken.
Stop pushing for a new start for us,
It's not going to happen, please no more push.

NATURE'S WAY OF LIVING

The hefty trees are tossed about, like seaweed on the foam,
Their branches reaching across like the antlers of a giant deer,
The leaves free-falling, like feathers from a thousand birds,
Carpeting the earth around, making cushions when you walk.
A rainbow of hues set before you, new ones appearing beneath the last,
Then cracking the twigs as each footstep comes down to rest.
So many wonderful sounds and smells, all your senses working as one,
This fragrance blends together, it's hard to tell them apart.
New noises from the forest underlay, creatures you never see.
There are so many trees, none of them matching their namesake:
That's the marvel of nature, so unalike, yet all with their own beauty.
I wish there was the same in people; instead we lose splendour with age.
But if you look hard and long enough we have answers like the forest.

ILLUSTRATION BY JUDI LAMB

REGRETS OF A LOVER

When that special person bows out of your life,
Whatever you try, the emptiness is impossible to fill.
Because of mistiming she never became your wife,
Back then the non-occasion was both your will.

The happiness is found and then stupidly cast away,
Usually one partner doesn't realise until too late.
A different field, a greener grass, eventually turning hay,
You have carved the milestone of your own fate.

Having everything in your grasp, then releasing your hand,
Frantically searching as you sink deeper in the bottomless
    pool,
Breaking the hourglass of your world, blinded by the sand,
Desperate fingers clasping grains of love, the actions of a
    fool.

We can all look back at our mindless mistakes,
Each one in turn wiser after the event.
More thought for two, not you, is what it takes,
Then to understand the love was heaven sent.

There is more to living than fun and games,
Two into one, I believe a possible division.
What good are goals and gilt-edged aims,
Not sharing the result makes pointless revision.

She'll always be there, with whom or wherever I be,
My well-being I know she chooses the best,
As I do for her, remembering, never would it be me,
Sitting alone like a bird in borrowed nest.

No one can destroy memories and photos in my brain,
The years will pass and my dreams will become few;
But the images of our love will forever remain,
Locked away with regrets and thoughts of you.

With emotions and passion the kisses we freely gave,
Warm feelings of tenderness felt for each other.
I hope in your mind and heart you're able to save
Some fragment of love, sheltered by one another.

So as time marches on, new mountains I'll scale,
To be healthy and happy in my own place.
Wherever I get to, uphill or down dale,
There will be a corner for your lovely face.

You've always believed that things happen with reason,
One morning I'll awake with answers, my lover and mate.
But for now it's no clearer with each changing season,
Still tears sore my eyes, sorrow, wrong decision, or fate.

EX AND WHY

When you see your ex-partner out with her new man,
You try and wish them good things the best way that you can.
Even though it hurts a little your head will make it stop,
But it's that nagging sub-conscious that just won't let it drop.
Your mind plays overtime as you are in semi-sleep in bed,
Thinking of what you said to her, and then what you should have said;
After all it was only yesterday you looked at the photos you had kept,
Thoughts of good times, are we foolish, how the dreams away we swept.
But she deserves true happiness, and realise this you could never give her.
You both tried many times, but the same old problems would re-occur,
She still looks lovely, radiant and full of fun,
Just like the first date, long ago, when your togetherness begun.

Yes, it's a strange feeling, seeing her and not wanting to be
　　there,
Friends on both sides watching you react, does he still
　　really care?
That goes without question; she'll be a part of me 'til my
　　dying day,
This I know with hand on heart, I know she'll never feel the
　　same way.
I gave a thought to her on New Year's Eve, and did she
　　think of me as well?
Now I'll never know, and even so she's not the type that
　　would tell.
No use dwelling on what we had; my time has gone and
　　passed me by,
I hope to God we'll still remain friends when all the hurts
　　run dry.
You can't help thinking is he good for her, but then she
　　looked happy you must agree,
And maybe one day the right person will come along, and
　　she'll be good for me.

THE JOYS OF DRIVING

Has the whole world gone mad?
Turning our pleasure into sad?
I'm talking about driving on the road,
People asking, 'What's a Highway Code?'
Let's overtake on the motorway,
Because my slip road is seconds away,
So it's dangerous to get past this car,
I'll be home two minutes before you, Ha! Ha!
Kamikaze pilots behind a black wheel,
Why so slow? What's the big deal?
Get round this bend, then a pint in The Crown,
Oh my God! That's why they're slowing down.
The law hiding to sentence speeding cars,
Rather than busying themselves with fights in bars,
Processions of roadworks making you late,
Temporary lights, endless minutes you wait.
Monster machinery like big yellow dragons,
Devouring our roads to fill up the wagons.
What happened to that long pleasant drive?
Thank God for mobiles: 'I don't know when we'll arrive'.
Some drivers won't reach the old age of thirty;
Courtesy, road sense, these actions are dirty.
At last a lovely quiet country lane:
Why the traffic jam? Oh! Please, it's insane.
Back to horse and carts, more contentment by far,
But then some genius idiot would invent the car.

ILLUSTRATION BY MICK BROWN

HOTPOT OF LIFE

Emotions close to boiling in the cauldron of my
    mind,
    Then someone regulates to simmer when
    they're feeling kind.
    Each tap we turn at different times when we've
had enough,
But even with these there is no control when it gets really
    tough.
If we knew the answers, then in life no one of us would ever
    fail,
The thing is we need failure to succeed, otherwise it
    becomes unreal.

Half-baked ideas cooked to perfection, they rise only to
    fall,
Dreams set on fire, roasted to ashes, leaving a charcoal
    wall.
From the smoke and the embers we build more notions to
    be hurled,
Steaming our way through life, a bright new venture for the
    world.
This is the one, I can't believe it, the thoughts bubble to the
    top,
No barriers as yet, still brewing, now the lid is ready to
    pop.
My wildest hopes redeemed, all that's past was worthwhile,
The vapours flow, like a stew that comes together in
    tremendous style.
Many offers of financial aid come seeping in every day,
You're on your way, you need nothing, just luxuries all the
    way.
A millionaire now, more friends than you remember,
    happiness just glows,
Expensive tastes, designer clothes, pounds on your figure,
    and it shows.
You've worked hard for this, so what's it matter? I've got it
    all here;
Is this what you've strived for? Headaches with worry,
    same year after year.
Do something, instead of growing old like the valued
    copper kettle,
Phone a friend, yes I'll pay, rich meal, eventually my ulcer
    will settle.
Give it away if it's not what you want, or go and find a
    partner to share it,
Let your feelings fry, your ideas boil; dreams once again,
    like the oven, are lit.

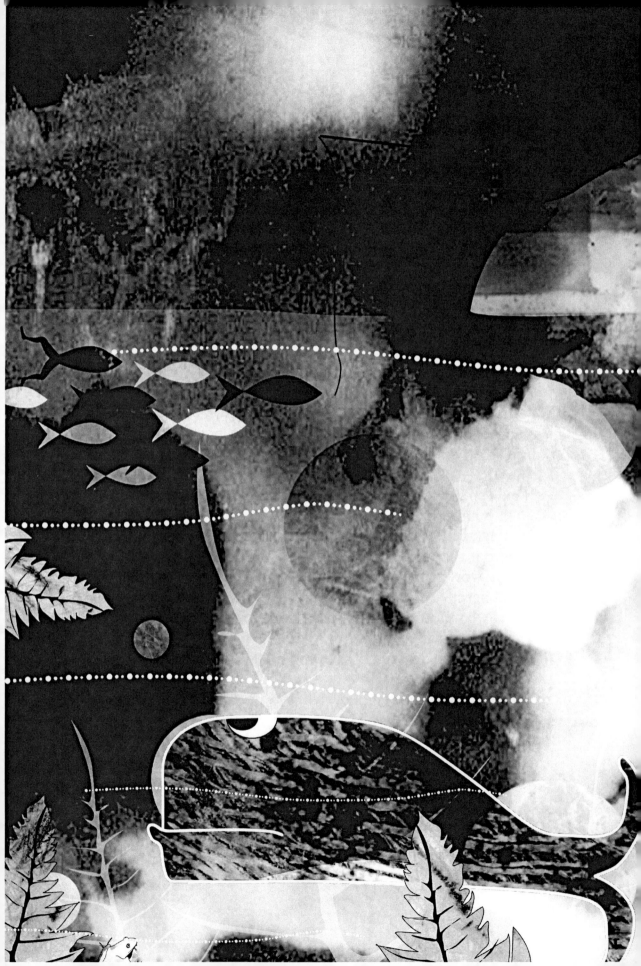

KNOWLEDGE OF OUR WATERS

As we search through the film of the river's
moving surface
Into a whole world of wonderment, deep among
plants peculiar,
The trout threading their way amidst fern-
shaped leaves,
Many colours of the rainbow speckled across the fish,
Smooth river stones awash with broken anglers' floats and
hooked lines,
Minuscule bodies and tadpoles shimmering by, untouched
by larger inhabitants,
Frogs and toads breast-stroking up towards the warm
sunlight,
Beetles of all sizes darting here, there and everywhere,
Not really looking as they know or care where they're
heading,
The undercurrent carrying the debris along, tossing it
around as if sorting it out,
River beds concealing years of secrets that will never be
revealed,
Millions of layers of life through the rampages of time.
Unlike the canals, the rivers and brooks we have the deep
mass of the sea,
Hiding common, also unknown creatures to man and beast,
Like another continent littered with barnacled wrecks and
ruins,
Gentle mammals the size of ocean-going vessels minding
their own business,
Then sometimes killers when disturbed, earning a history
of destruction.

ILLUSTRATION BY NICKI ALGAR

Talk of prehistoric existence lower than man has dared to
    venture,
Treasures and rewards of every source hidden away in
    caverns and coral,
Yet another marvel of our planet, all this, even the smallest
    wet being
Can survive surrounded by water without touching dry
    land;
Even men need to call on artificial means to live in this
    world of water.
But how did the population beneath the rippling calm and
    mighty waves evolve?
Maybe they once walked and with time lost limbs through
    lack of use,
Or to become land-living developed legs and eventually
    staggered to ground.
At the end of the day we'll never realise how it was all
    created,
As long as we absorb the wonders of watery depths, never
    underestimating this amazing universe.

A CAPTIVE IN YOUR OWN HEART

Many times the game is played,
Hurting deeply a third party involved.
Slowly edges of hearts become frayed,
Days holding you prisoner, nothing solved.
New hope shedding light on the affair,
Could this be the moment you've prayed for?
A piercing gaze into her eyes, love is there,
She holds you tight, kissing you just once more.

You feel it's right but then to part,
Sadly a captive in your own heart.

When you next meet days have been lost,
Trying to rekindle that weakened flame.
It burns once more bright, but what cost;
She leaves again, your lips trace her name.

Your body knows it was meant to start,
Changing emotion, a captive in your own heart.

You know a final decision will be sought,
Denial of true love, this road it will follow.
Questioning how else could I have fought?
Lumps in your throat make it impossible to swallow,

What you had to offer, not enough for her,
Loving each other forever, though apart.
The lonely years ahead without this partner,
Still bound, a captive in your own heart,

Knowing what to expect when she returns,
Yet her back is facing on her new life,
Leaving a confused soul that desperately yearns,
For this exciting lady to end the strife.

She too feels a painful loving dart,
Destined to be a captive in her own heart.

PIECES OF LIFE

L ife is like a game of chess,
Think your moves or it becomes a mess.
To begin with birth we are the pawn,
Taking our first steps soon after we're born.
Obstacle ahead, we move diagonally across,
This is a way forward to show who's boss.
We jump with the knight, then step to the side,
This cautious act we manoeuvre with pride.
The holy bishop moves diagonally on the board,
This, like religion, is sometimes ignored.
The rook is so solid, horizontally it goes,
This is the path in life that we chose.
The regal queen has the whole board to compete,
If you reach this stage the world's at your feet.
The noble king totters sadly, at a time one square,
He can't be removed, but one must be aware.
The game moves on through the barriers of age,
Until you're stopped in your tracks, checked at this stage.
The pieces move freely, some become friends,
Several pass away, whilst others make amends.
Which direction do you stroll along this playing field?
Forever being halted, expected at times to yield.
The king's partner, she guards him lovingly to the end,
But alas is overpowered, several rivals they send.
The noble monarch is cornered; checkmate is at hand,
Maybe not a bad thing, there's peace throughout the land.
So next time you play this most thoughtful game,
Remember through life, we behave just the same.

ILLUSTRATION BY ANDY FIRTH

BEER, GEAR AND EAR ARE HERE

Is the answer to sink numerous quarts of ale?
To become known as a definite macho male?
Because, believe me, the looks you get are chronic
If you order mineral water or a ginless tonic.
I think it's more in the north that people demand
A man can't stand at the bar without a pint in his hand.
No matter how long you know a friend the offer's always
    there,
'What would you like with it? Have a drink if you dare.'
'I've a full glass,' you reply, 'I'm enjoying it as well,'
So order what I ask for, or please just go to hell.

If a man wears pastel shades, shocking pink springs to mind,
The night club's Hercules and Goliath whispering, 'Hmm,
    we know his kind'.
Why should he-men ridicule others for clothes of orange
    and yellow?
Are these muscle-bound blockheads not knowing it takes
    more to be a fellow?
I like blue, also black, but I'm not afraid of wearing a
    different hue,
Even mates can't take bright colours. 'What you come as?'
    Right on cue.
I put it down to insecurity of the less adventurous males,
'Some of us can look good in anything' – this answer never fails,
But at the end of the day it's up to the individual what he wears,
Polka dots, stripes or flowers – if he's a great guy, who
    cares?

ILLUSTRATION BY PAUL PARKES

I remember as a kid admiring my mum's earrings, drops of
    pearls,
Many shapes and sizes, sparkling jewels from beneath the
    curls,
Thinking then why would anybody have holes drilled
    through their ears,
Why inflict pain on oneself, and choose to end up in tears?
But now the world's gone mad, nowhere on the body
    escapes,
Rows of rings, chains and studs displayed like metal
    drapes.
As though this wasn't bad enough, nipples, eyebrows and
    lips
Pierced in abundance, also penis, vaginas with silver grips.
I saw a sight the other day, a ringed tongue, please don't
    choke.
My eyes fixed on the adorned mouth and yes, it was a
    bloke.

PEOPLE'S VOICE

As you enter the smoke-filled bar
You won't get very far,
The crowd is six men deep,
All there to get a peep
At the lady on the stage,
Who has tempered all the rage.
The songs she sings with style,
Entertaining all the while,
Folks come from miles around
To hear the group with the big sound,
The band strikes up once more
As she dances on the floor,

She's the singer in the band,
With such power in her voice,
She's the singer in demand,
The people's latest choice.

Covering the stage and in control
Of love songs, soul and rock and roll,
Her voice fills the room again,
Loud cheers; yes! Mostly men.
Passions are high, emotions reeling,
The applause, raising the ceiling.

She's the singer in the spotlight,
A dream to all the guys;
She's the singer in the dim light,
Hiding sadness in her eyes.

She's the singer in the band,
And she makes the stage her own.
She's the singer in demand,
Yet she wanders home alone.

ILLUSTRATION BY SUSAN TIDSWELL

MUMS, BLESS 'EM!

A mum keeps you warm and safe when you're small,
Then later repairs and patches you up, each time you fall.
A watchful eye when you're out playing with your mates,
Proud to pick you up, outside the school gates,
Listening to your adventures on the way home,
Brushing your hair, gentle hands for a comb.
They wrapped you in crossed scarves, mittens and a silly woollen hat,
You can laugh at those far-off days, now you know you looked a prat.
No longer a child, she's there to see you grow,
Proud as a peacock and lets everyone know.
Now in your teens, a tough time for her,
You know it all, that's when arguments occur;
But if you stood back and listened for a while,
You'd see she was right, once again; there's that smile.

The years pass by, and girlfriends come and go,
She calls them all love, 'cause their names she doesn't
    know.
Struggles and worries she bares, like everyone on earth,
But she hides these moments from you, for all she is
    worth.
There have been times I've watched her, bewildered she's
    there,
After all she's put up with why should she still care?
For mums this is simple, they forgive whatever,
When you take time to think you realise who's clever.
Hugs, love and cuddles are free, you've had them all your
    life.
If you get married, you'll get more from a loving wife.

A mum lets you go, whilst keeping a firm hold.
Still offering advice and remedies for that cold.
Your hardships encountered, she's there in the wings,
Tears, relationships, problems, her help she still brings.
We can never repay all the many things they've done
    for us,
All the times we've tried, we're told 'stop making a fuss'.
To try to fathom out why mums do what they do
Would take someone wiser than me and maybe you.
I think when you're born they look down with baited breath,
Deciding this is their role in life, looking after you 'til death.
Ask a mum what she wants, the answer's always the same,
'I've got everything I need the day I gave you your name.'
When you get older this mum can also be a mate,
And you could kick yourself realising this too late.
So mums are a breed apart, irreplaceable you must agree,
These miracles of nature, the making of you and me.
After all I've said about this journey of life I must sum,
Let's be truly honest, guys, would you choose to be a
    mum?

TRUTH REVEALED, STILL HIDDEN

When your heart searches for a simple clue
To an answer that totally escapes you,
Where do you find the strength to go on fighting?
As all around the teeth of love are biting.
Friends all say you must get a life somehow;
They don't realise your insides are in a constant row.
Deep down you know it's the right course to choose,
Whichever path you take the result is you will lose.
The turmoil in your mind could cause it to explode,
Like a well-oiled machine, programmed to overload.
You can't live with her for reasons beyond your control,
And to be without her will cripple you to your soul,
Yet you have to sacrifice the precious love you share,
Knowing the tremendous hurt and scars you leave there,
If only you could delve deep inside your aching head,
To find solutions to the questions, the answers you dread.
Each waking day you try to charge your bewildered brain,
Scanning every angle, then back to square one again.
Most problems you have tackled through life whilst getting
    old,
But this has got you beat if truth be known and told.
To love her is to leave her, it seems easy, the written word,
Truth to oneself to leave her, when you love her is absurd.

How can you go through life when the past months are
    hard to take?
You've got to be strong and for both of you make a clean
    break:
The plans you made in your head are with you and going
    nowhere.
If they were possible for her I'm sure these with you she'd
    share.
Do you wait patiently in the wings for the outcome of her
    life to see,
Or do you pack your heart in a suitcase and move far away
    so gallantly?
You've sought advice of others and know what most say is
    right,
Then why do you feel so empty and tortured day and
    night?
This paragraph of lonely love no doubt will close the final
    chapter,
The willpower you have to draw, for you is painful for long
    after.
To wish you were a child again with clear thoughts and not
    a care,
But if that were true, you'd never have experienced her
    being there.

PEOPLE, THAT'S US

What funny beings we people are,
This island of ours and countries afar,
Living in boxes of all shapes and size,
Searching for a larger one, next pay rise.
We decorate them with assorted colours and hues,
Hoping new buildings will not spoil our views.
When inside we stare at a box changing pictures,
Wondering what to do next with fittings and fixtures,
Important to impress our family and friends
With all the new styles and the latest trends;
There's no stopping us with everything we see.
That's a lovely dog, ours is pedigree,
What a fantastic new, oh! secondhand car,
Well, just another week for my new Jaguar.
I heard from a friend you have a brand new TV,
When you have time look at my fifty inch plasma with HD.
There's no end to this snobbery and greed,
Right down to the newspapers we read.
Cornwall was nice, but Fiji was great,
Winning the lottery I believe was fate.
I can't remember the last time we had corned beef hash,
Our favourite's M&S steak and ale pie with a mint buttered
    mash.
The central cooker's a dream, how's your stove?
No, we flew here; I can't believe that you drove.
We pass the ritual onto our kids without a care:
Designer labels, logos, latest mobiles, Nike footwear.
This goes on from the crib to the ground;
Not news: a solution doesn't want to be found.

THERE'S NEVER AN EASY WAY

You'll know when this moment arrives
By the tingling you get from inside,
The excitement you feel from her touch,
Her kisses move you, oh! so much.
When you're lost in these feelings of love
Your heart flies free like a dove,
The pleasure and tenderness you get
You keep from the moment you met.

How do you know when you're right?
Yes! In the middle of the night
When you turn your head and see
Your love sleeping silently,
It's got to be a feeling deep
Inside each one of us, asleep,
Then it takes that special one
Our eyes to open towards the sun.

There's never an easy way
To say what you have to say.
Loving isn't hard we know,
Staying in love is, and watching it grow.

In life we see it all,
The hardships and the falls.
Love comes and goes through time,
Never knowing what we may find,
Everyone hoping that one day
The perfect partner will come their way.
It's the hardest thing on earth
To truly love for all it's worth.

THE LADY'S DECISION

Yes, she has a dream
While asleep and so serene;
She has a love for life,
And maybe one day she'll be a wife.
Her face doesn't show the worry
When enjoying and making merry,
Should she go home at once and pack,
And take a near future flight back,
Or stay at the home she's made,
Because she is good at her chosen trade?
Aside from this, there's always a loved one,
Is it worth leaving to follow the sun?
You never know, he may answer her prayers some day;
How would she hear him if she was so far away?
This lovely female has so much love to give,
And we hope one day, for herself, she starts to live,
She knows we'll help her in any way we can,
Even into the arms of a selected man.
Happiness she deserves, as much as anyone we know,
Love, care, trust and respect all to grow.
The answer to her dream lies deep within,
To take those first steps to freedom is for her to begin.
When the bubble bursts, with no wall to guide her,
We'll be there as always with comfort, yes sir.

DADS, RESPECT 'EM!

Who was it that made splendid castles in the sand,
With flags and moats and four turrets alike,
The man that steered you with a steady hand,
Trust you showed him on your first new bike.

This is a dad who loved you like no other,
Sometimes sharing love with sister or brother.

Remember being carried on broad shoulders aloft,
Feeling like a giant, reaching for the sky?
Tucking you in bed, with strong hands, yet soft,
At times reading fairytales that made you cry.

This is a dad whom you are getting to know,
Proud as a peacock, his child to show.

He taught you to swim, but not out of sight
Until you were confident to go it alone,
Occasionally checking your homework is right,
First day he watched you go to school on your own.

This is a dad who worked hard every day,
All the hours God sent, very little pay.

Once in your teens, not showing the earned respect,
All your mates saying this is the thing to do,
The good times you shared, now seeming to neglect,
Forgetting this great man, always there for you.

This is a dad, who taught you wrong from right,
Gently pleased your later years were in sight.

Then came the day you passed your driving test,
You were proud he helped you choose your first car,
Wishing those teenage years you hadn't digressed,
Glad to be the kid of the best guy you'd met by far.

This is a dad who took you for your first drink,
Knowing that it wasn't, but this he let you think.

The years pass by, and this man becomes a mate,
Laughing, chatting, learning things you never knew,
Why this wondrous friendship you left so late,
Realising, now older, he was waiting for you.

This is a dad, providing for family all the years,
Him and Mum working, never showing his fears.

You get married and have children of your own,
The cycle begins again, now Grandad to the new,
Watch from distance as your loved ones are shown
Love that you were given, but not taken from you.

This is a dad, a mighty oak since your life began,
Shame he never heard the words, 'Dad, I'm your biggest
    fan.'

JUST GIVE ME HOPE

The memories you gave me
Are branded in my heart,
Disillusioned promises
That we would never, never part
If there was someone new
This I could understand,
I've been this way before,
But this is foreign land.

Just give me hope, just send a word,
A little note, however absurd,
Just please say yes, or just say no,
A simple sign; I never saw you go.

The plans we made together
Seem so distant in the past.
The track we saw before us
We vowed would last and last.

The life we built
Was it all in vain?
I know they were dreams
But they still remain.
I hope you shed a tear
When you think of me.
From within I fear,
But you don't hear my plea.

A VOICE TO NOWHERE

Her talent is rare,
Many times she's been told,
But she doesn't care,
Her career she will fold,
A god-given gift
Should make her proud
Never to shift
This decision, so loud.
We all try in vain,
Yet to no avail,
'Please sing again',
Though we all fail.
Years that lie ahead
Are hard we know,
She'll remember what's said,
Wishing she'd had a go.
We can't all be wrong,
Still she won't hear,
Her will is so strong,
Our message is clear.

Can she not see?
The feelings she brings
To all who are free
Each time she sings.
If the passion has gone
We can do no more,
A star could have shone,
Of this we're all sure.
But if this she doesn't need,
Then who are we to say?
We've helped to plant the seed,
Hope it blossoms one day;
So if it's not meant to be,
Because no more she gets the buzz,
Then all the people agree
She'll succeed in whatever she does.

TWO PEOPLE AS ONE HEART

If I could have seen how much you meant to me,
Instead of the fool I've been, thinking someone else had
the key.
The stupid things I did, the stupid games I played,
The trust that I destroyed, no wonder you're afraid.
Experience, it is said, comes to you with age,
Like all the books I've read, I long for the next page.

Two people as one heart, two people as one heart,
Two people as one heart, what to do when it breaks apart.

I realise now, always too late for it to matter,
The joy we have lost, the life I came to shatter,
The home we called our own, the work we did together,
The tears in your eyes, when our 'for always' became a
    'never'.
I've always myself to blame, but believe me when I say
There will never be another I could love in the same way.

Once more we try again to heal the open scars,
The pain it may not show, like the tyre marks of cars.
But the closer that you look the tread is there to see,
Like the pain, the hurt, the worry and wishing to be free.
Now we have the passion, the words we try to believe,
The motions of being in love, are we able to retrieve.

ILLUSTRATION BY ANDREA STEVENSON

DENIAL OF LIFE

When you're treated badly and you know not why,
Because all you've shown is love, respect and devotion,
You search your mind for answers, ending in a sigh,
There seems no justice for this new-found explosion.

To admit to oneself that it's over, not to last,
Is one of the hardest things there is to see through,
When your head is flooded with memories near past,
Strange thoughts of what now is left for you.

If you see her again you know your heart will race,
Is this the right thing to do or will it hurt you more?
There are no answers, these questions you must face,
Maybe when they are solved, you'll feel somewhat secure.

What have I done to be tortured in this way?
Am I being punished for old loves that I did wrong?
Only God knows this, but I wish he was able to say,
So I could find some reason why the pain drags along.

I'm told one thing and then another; which is right?
I possibly trust too easily, loving words this is true.
If only I could grasp onto one thing then I'd fight
To keep our love in bloom, for the future me and you,

Once again a waiting game, the decision is not mine,
How long can a man hold on to what he believes in?
Will it be the phone, or hopefully a visit is the sign,
Whatever she chooses, fingers crossed for your new begin,

If time she has taken to absorb the love and truth spoken,
Then surely we must spend our lives lovingly together,
Unless I've been fooled and the promises are there to be
    broken.
If this is so, then all I have are my magical moments forever.

You can only deny yourself so much in life's dream,
True happiness does not call on you every day you live.
To say we'd have it all, plus strawberries and cream,
Would be false, but the fruit we'd have would be ours to
    give.

MODERN DAY GLADIATORS

Many brave hearts arrive at the end of flight,
With numerous sport bags the nations unite.
The nerve-racking time of getting through round one,
Fighting the butterflies, the battle's begun.
Backhand, forehand, rapid serve yet again,
Chips, lobs, slices, separating boys from men.
The green grass of Wimbledon in all its glory,
New roof, awaiting two weeks to tell its story.
Gladiators exchanging sword, shield and spear
For well-strung rackets, overcoming all fear.
Christians and lions spring quickly to mind,
Each warrior their opponent's weakness to find.
The tantrums, the grunts, the balls that are out,
We're in for a close one, of this there's no doubt.
A smash to the corner, it's just in, then a sigh,
Baited breath, the decision from hawkeye.

Tiebreakers keeping you on the edge of your seat,
Pounding ball after ball in this scorching heat,
Thousands of fans screaming for their choice,
Each one trying to be the loudest voice.
Male and female courageous in their fights,
All displaying splendour in their chosen whites,
Bravado and nerve shown at such a young age,
These giants of the court attempting the next stage.
The stamina and fitness, amazing maturity,
Needing the wins for later life security.
Games and matches come and go away,
The victor living to fight another day.
Now the second week, surprises remaining,
For the few it's paid off, intensive training.
The finals are here, the skills you applaud,
Then the last set score, to reap the award.
The trophy held proud, engraved is the name,
At times it may read several years the same.
But whoever's triumphant, you all must agree,
An exhausting fortnight for us on the settee.

WHAT'S AGE ANYWAY? AS LONG AS YOU CAN PLAY

Why should chums be the same size and age,
And not enjoy words from any written page?
To play games and chat about what you care,
Be silly and laugh, these moments are rare.
The mind of a child is a wonderful thing,
To be treated as equal, the joy this can bring.
Watching telly and films together as one,
Mimicking characters, new voices, such fun.
Each other's company for meals, what to eat,
The smiles we both give each time we meet.
This pal of mine is forty years less than me,
But that doesn't matter, this she doesn't see.
The times that we have, we end up playing the fool,
No doubt she tells her mates when she goes into school.
Making one another happy, looking to the next time,
Because of our birthdays of the same zodiac sign.
Maybe this is another reason we get on so well,
She is my tresured friend, I think she is swell.
We've laughed 'til we've cried on many a night,
The companionship between us for us is just right.
Mastermind, Chinese chequers, monopoly and now chess,
I treat her as a young adult, she wouldn't expect less.
If I let her win this would not teach her at all,
So when she beats me with pride it makes her feel tall.
Hoping our friendship goes on, whatever occurs,
I'll not break the bond, the decision will be hers.
I trust her visits will go on some time at length,
The pleasure we get from them gives us both strength.
Jokes we play, our sense of humour makes us elate -
Yes! These are just a few things I get from my young mate.

ILLUSTRATION BY ALEX MENSTON

JOHN AND MEL, TOGETHER SO WELL

As I arrived too early the sun was just breaking through,
I strolled around the garden taking in the picturesque view.
Amidst the peace and serenity I espied a garden swing,
I promptly lay down to rest, listening to the morning birds sing.
My eyes soon closed, a deep sleep, as I swung to and fro,
A soft gentle breeze, I awoke, hearing my name called out low.
Raising my head, John greeted me, with the warmth he'd shown all my life;
Hello! Come in and there was lovely Mel, very soon to be his wife.
A cup of tea, chatting about this and that, looking around their wonderful abode,
Each room their character filled, they were proud and oh! how it showed.
It's a dream come true, they've worked so hard, no-one deserves more than this loving pair,
I'm so glad to be invited, sharing their home, and felt that they were pleased I was there.
As the day wore on we talked of the plans for their extra-special day;
Taking the keys, I washed the car, and then gently placed it away.
We talked some more, then relaxed after being so well fed,
It was so pleasant an evening, and now we were ready for bed.

Morning light, plenty to do, a few precious moments resting
on the sofa,

I felt good, they looked great, I was proud to be their acting
chauffeur.

The service went smoothly, and I had time to reflect on
partners that might have been;

Back to earth, they weren't meant to be. My old mate John,
gazing at Mel, his Queen.

The guests they arrived, a mixed group they were, each with
different tales to tell,

With Eric and Rene, Emma and John, Richard, Carla and
Hannah all getting on so well.

The champagne flowed, the happiness grew, stories from
young and old,

Excellent food, the cameras flashed, a shame the merriment
has to fold.

The washing up done, away it was cleared; time to look
back on a memorable day,

I wouldn't have missed it, and I know we'll fondly remember
the twenty-seventh of May.

Looking at the two of them cuddled up, I believe their
togetherness was fate,

I've known John a long time, he's a good friend, and now I
saw Mel a new mate.

WHO'S MAURICE? WHO'S CHRIS? YOU'LL KNOW MORE WHEN YOU'VE READ THIS

This bloke I met over two score years and some,
Through all our school time, when he decided to
come.
An independent, controversial being, who only
sees black and white,
Now and then on a listening mood he may see things in
another light.
As a mate he was always there, in battle and in peace,
When the odds were against him, you had to tell him to
cease.
His education was found, tatting, gypsies, dealing,
streetwise in life,
Then at a tender age responsibility, along came Christine
his new wife.
'I'm a man' was the caption we gave him in his wedding
photograph,
With bubbly Chris and stone-faced Mo; even now we look at
this and laugh.
At first it was a struggle, but soon they came into their own,
With the reality of one, and the gritty rock that had grown.
Many a year went by, now with a young bairn to feed as
well,
But together they were solid, unruffled, get on, 'what the
hell',
Working with coarse stone, some say a rough diamond, but
he is not
I admit a granite surface, but a soft centre is what he's got.

Later on a sad blow he was dealt, leaving him with a broken
　　back,
Even covered in plaster, crumbling at front, to make love
　　they found the knack,
But joking aside, what would they do, a complete turnabout
　　was in the making,
I'd like to think that I had a hand in the new direction they
　　would be taking.
I've had many years away, and our paths we have walked
　　apart,
No matter, these two are my roots, and we give each other
　　heart.
He swears, she has an infectious laugh, and talks of his
　　wide girth!
The welcome mat is always there. Yes! They are the salt of
　　the earth.

We respect each other in what we've done and green is
　　never an issue,
The dialogue flows, the truth is spoken of lies, there is no
　　tissue.
Eggs and bacon, bread and butter, Maurice and Chris,
　　these two are as one,
And all the qualities, and many more besides, are moulded
　　in their son.
This man's ideas and thoughts you may not agree with in
　　any way,
Whatever the subject be, he believes in this, he'll never sway.
His animals and birds are a part of life to him that is dear,
He handles their every need, and finishes the day with a
　　beer.
The artistic side of his partner is a pleasure you have to
　　behold,
Gentle brush strokes in her paintings, like she worked with
　　silver and gold.

Through hardships, illness, strife, she's come through with
    flying colours,
All the things they've toiled for, unfortunately envied by
    several others.
These are failings that can be seen from people that will
    choose to be blind.
With time, effort, together in love, they are two or one of a
    kind.
I've only skimmed the edge, but this is where my writing
    ends,
Throughout all the years, to sum it up, I've loved Mo and
    Chris, my friends.

SPIKE

I only knew Spike for a short time really,
But on first meeting we were buddies clearly.
We laughed and chatted and shared a joke
In between drinks and yet another smoke.
His voice was like velvet at the keyboard alone,
Making everyone welcome with his dulcet tone.
The songs that he sang came from him with ease,
Audiences of plenty, their ears he did please.
His fingers skipped the keys with relish and zest,
No doubt from the people that he was the best.
A joy to listen to, and watch on the stage,
Ballads and jazz, the blues he'd engage.
To say he was cool is understating it's true,
Our precious times together, respect grew and grew.
The twinkle in his eye, the wise sideways grin,
Made you feel that he could read you from within.
He had done it, seen it and bought the T-shirt,
I wish I could have done more to release his hurt.
The cafés and bars where he will be sadly missed,
Remembering only good times, hearts he had kissed.
With love and respect I will remember this man,
These magical moments, we all truly can.
Several times I had the privilege to sing by his side,
He carried me through, the words we delivered with pride.
Spike and Brenda will go on forever, hand in hand,
With love in their hearts, everyone can understand.
Apart they may be, but that time is now,
 They'll find each other again, somehow.
There's lots more to say, and no one could rescind,
The voice of the island, our mate Spike, the true 'Summer Wind'.

DON, BUT NOT GONE

I've thought long and hard about writing this,
About a friend whom I'll really miss,
In 'Strangers' we were good mates,
Chatting whenever and having long debates.

Myself, Derek, Gordon, Maurice, Ian and Don,
'Escaped from the dark' and into the sun,
The ponies we handled, way down in the mine,
But above ground we couldn't keep them in line.

The drinks that we drank, the cigs that were smoked,
Our miners' black faces, the hours we joked.
Just this one job was a pleasure to work on,
With Alistair, Peter, Leslie, Joe and reliable Don.

Unfortunately we never worked together again,
But he got me a role in 'My Brother Jonathan',
He was unable to do this character part,
So he suggested me, right at the start.

We've had the same agents throughout our careers,
And long telephone calls over the years,
We would moan about this and laugh about that,
You could guarantee with Don, you'd have an interesting
    chat.

There was no-one worked harder in this profession,
The rewards he reaped were jobs in succession.
All the letters he wrote, all the calls he made,
Brought an abundance of roles and with skills he displayed.

The ideas would flow like wine, whilst seated in the pub,
The trouble from TV companies, accepting 'Paradise Club',
The business we'd question, sometimes shedding doubt,
Then thanking our lucky stars that we were 'Making Out'.

With his 'Bulman'-like face and his worn denim jacket,
His caring for people and the French gauloise packet,
The respect of fellow actors, and a pal you could depend,
Don, I sure as hell miss you, I'm so proud to call you
    friend.

THE ARTISTS

The Artists Who Have Contributed to Moods, Moments & Memories

Alexandra Menston
After studying foundation art and design I went on to gain a Higher National Diploma and then graduated with a BA Hons from the University of Westminster. I now work on diverse briefs using a wide range of media in fashion, textile, illustration and painting.
Poems Illustrated: Head and Heart, Each Plays a Part/Alone in Love/What's Age Anyway? As Long As You Can Play.
Contact: amenston@yahoo.com

Susan Tidswell
I was brought up in Carleton in Craven, but later moved to Skipton in Yorkshire; the gateway to the Yorkshire Dales. The beautiful hills of the Dales provided the inspiration to trigger my love for drawing. I now live in Bradford near my two children; Andrew (34) and Helen (27), and my two beautiful granddaughters, Bethany and Lauren. My love of drawing means I am often sketching from my window, as well as being inspired by a range of other scenes.
Poems Illustrated: Stress / People's Voice
Contact: catsue57@yahoo.co.uk

Andy Firth
After studying A-level art at school I decided to ditch all my ideas of working as a graphic designer and join a band! I started playing keyboards at the tender age of seven and went to play keyboards and Hammond organ professionally for ten years with some old friends from school. I still write and record music in my studio at home and live a happy life with my fiancé; Helen and our two beautiful daughters; Bethany and Lauren. This is my first piece of commissioned art and I have thoroughly enjoyed working on it.
Poem Illustrated: Pieces of Life
Contact: fuzzboxmanagement@live.co.uk

Paul Parkes
I am a student studying Virtual Reality Design with Animation at the University of Huddersfield. I like to draw in Flash and create my own character designs. My ultimate goal is to work for Pixar or Dreamworks Studios.
Poems Illustrated: Beer, Gear and Ear are Here / Journeying at Home
Contact: pp_hiphopdontstop@hotmail.co.uk
Website: http://parkespages.blogspot.com

Andrea Stevenson
I studied Graphic Design and Illustration at Bradford Art College from 1980 to 1984. My previous work includes illustrations for *The Dark Uniquiet Hills, Down at Beans Cafe* and *Bread and Circuses.* I have also done artwork for various posters and album/CD covers, murals and portraits. I am now studying photography in my spare time.
Poems Illustrated: A Pleasure to be Guilty / How The Worm Turns / Two People As One Heart
Contact: andreastevenson19@yahoo.co.uk

Simon Wray
Poem illustrated: What Is It?
Contact: pieface@gmail.com

Nicki Algar
Poem Illustrated: Knowledge of Our Waters
Contact: nicki.algar@thisisbrandnew.com

Dani Batty
Poem Illustrated: Full Circle
Contact: dani.batty@logistik.co.uk

Helen Knowles
Poem Illustrated: Aloha People
Contact: helenjknowles@hotmail.com

Mick Brown
Poems Illustrated: Hotpot of Life / Joys of Driving
Contact: mick@mickbrown.fsnet.co.uk

Christine Willan
Poems Illustrated: Whats is Love? / County Scars
Contact: 01274 652502

Judi Lamb
Poem Illustrated: Natures Way of Living

Lightning Source UK Ltd.
Milton Keynes UK

171454UK00001B/9/P